Butterfly

Butterfly Writer

Cheryl Hart

Copyright © 2022 by Cheryl Hart.
All rights reserved.

TAOW Press, 24 Sebring Avenue, Northop Hall, Wales, UK, CH7 6NP

Email TAOW Press: taowpress@gmail.com

ISBN: 9798810550860

First published 14th March 2022

Contents

Introduction	7
What is Wholehearted Writing?	19
Key Principles of Wholehearted Writing	35
Every Writer's Worst Enemy	49
You Are Enough	69
Recognising Your Value	81
Wholehearted Reading	93
Making Wholehearted Connections	105
Expand the Flow of Creativity	121
Cultivating a Leader Spirit	133

Dedication

For everyone with a dream that seems bigger than they are. Rise up to meet it.

Cheryl Hart

Introduction
Butterfly Writer

"The only important thing in a book is the meaning that it has for you."

W. Somerset Maugham

As an author, writing coach and editor I have had my fair share of writing positions. I have read countless submissions of other people's written work, and I have found that the best connections between writer and reader come from a place of wholeheartedness, understanding and an ability to relate to the topic in hand, and of course, the person that reads it. Butterfly writing is wholehearted writing that makes long lasting connections.

It should be remembered that writing is about connecting and creating meaning with transformational powers rather than flaunting a literary prowess that only few can understand.

I know some of you will be questioning your

right or your worth to write a book, and some of these insecurities may be driven from what you think makes great story-telling and whether you think that you fit into this category of a great story-teller. One of the most poignant aspects of writing is language, and I know many consider that their ability to articulate their story and the lessons within will hold them back. But what is the point of setting out to write a book if you choose words that keep the real you at a distance and your audience baffled? Literary prowess, in my opinion, is how well you engage with your audience through the way you tell your story in a relatable way. This is good story-telling. If your intention is to write a book so you can show off how well you can describe an autumnal scene; a scene that produces marvellous imagery using superfluous words that only a handful of people are familiar with, you're already at a loss. Yes, it will be evident that you can create beautiful prose to some readers, but others who read it may be left kicking up the leaves looking for the meaning beneath.

Without purpose, you will not complete the best story you're capable of, and perhaps without intention, you will alienate a number of your target audience. If you are writing a book with the intention to share experience, or are wanting to write a book for yourself to better understand that experience, then you should be aware from the beginning that it is with your heart and soul that you will write this book, not with fluffy literary prose – because a heart and soul in writing creates a book's purpose – and that purpose is for your readers to connect with. It is this purpose that must connect with the right audience, using appropriate language so that your story and your purposeful message can be understood universally. It is not that a portion of your potential readers will be stupid – it is because language is vast. Language covers many dialects across many regions, throughout varied systems of education and professions, each with its own set of familiar vocabulary.

As writers we can produce a narrative with a selection of words that educate readers as they come across them perhaps for the first time, but you must not choose language that alienates on a whole. Instead, choose simple language that is welcoming and inclusive. The reason I prompt you to use language that is comfortable for you, is because you will want to pass on this comfort to your reader. Language can create a barrier between reader and writer. Whilst you may have been faced with various reasons why you shouldn't write this book, I would like for you to disregard this reason right away. Writing intellect comes in different shapes and sizes, and choosing the right language will always depend on how well you know your audience. Books create connection, and this book will show you exactly what I mean by this, and discuss how you can achieve this.

Taking another example of writing into account for what wholehearted writing is not, is the click bait method that fills our devices. Media headlines inviting readers to 'click here' for more of a story generally has the depth of a puddle. Click bait has no love. It has no compassion. It has no empathy. It has no wisdom. At the heart of click bait you'll find a money machine with zero motivation to connect with a reader for more time than it takes for them to serve the sponsored adverts that fill its pages with interruption after interruption, finally leaving the viewer underwhelmed and unfulfilled. Click bait is the lowest form of trying to appeal to readers through hyperbolic headlines and ambiguity. The message you click for, you never usually get. The way in which you tell your story needs to be driven right from your heart for deeper connections that spark transformation in you and your reader. This is the essence of a butterfly writer.

I like to think readers are savvy individuals who are growing wiser to this fodder impressing on our daily lives. It is contrived manipulation to get you to part with your time to make them money. Most of us are guilty clickers passing the time and willingly click away. But the one thing that isn't being achieved through this relationship is a wholehearted connection. We're in danger of losing a wholehearted connection in our lives through the lack of social contact over the past few years with the growing fear of the pandemic, and the way technology dominates households. But that mustn't stop us from reaching out and connecting in every which way possible. Literature should open hearts and minds to new ways of seeing and doing things; and provide comfort that we're not alone in whatever we're feeling. Literature has the power to create change, alliance, solidarity, understanding, transformation and even self-love.

The way you choose to write and the subjects you choose to write about should sit somewhere between your heart and your soul. When you feel that warmth inside of your chest as you write - this is when you know that what you're writing is coming from the best place - a place of passion, honesty and purpose.

It takes a certain type of person to write click bait – I should know. I was one of them. My experience in this was short lived because the editor hated my heart and soul leaking into every article. For a large international corporation that receives 20 million website visitors per month, there was a particular robotic technique to producing this type of writing, and it had very little to do with writing from the heart to create long-lasting connections. Perhaps other content writers are yearning to put their heart and soul into meaningful writing. If this is you, then you're in the right place.

The strongest of messages often are the simplest ones, and yet, the idea of being a writer or author terrifies some. In some instances, aspiring authors may think that their vocabulary isn't strong enough, that they should understand circa 171,000 words that make up the *Oxford Dictionary*. Well, I'm here to tell you, this isn't the case. As you will discover through reading the chapters within this book, the language you use is fundamentally who you are. It is how you identify with the world around you and how the world identifies with you. Sure, grab a dictionary and a thesaurus to broaden your knowledge and find that perfect word that sums up what you want to say, but it's incredibly important to own who you are and where you come from and the language that's familiar to you. Regardless of whether you think you're worth it, I can tell you right now, that you are. All you need to do is learn how to access your heart voice and tell your story through it. And whilst it's always good to learn new words and ways to communicate, it is not necessary to change who you are and the words you use to be accepted as a writer and the author of your story. Ultimately, this would be denying your sense of self and avoiding the real you. It is your heart the reader is invested in knowing. Trust that and let it be enough.

Today, I came across a quote that read "The only important thing in a book is the meaning that it has for you." This quote is by far one of the best quotes I have ever read when it comes to what can be said about a book. If you make the choice to avoid putting yourself (your whole heart) on the page, you may as well not bother writing the story yourself. Without putting your whole self into something you risk your message not being authentic, and when pieces are missing, the story is incomplete.

Will it be easy? No. With it be worth it? Always.

Learning to open up from a place of wholeheartedness will present its own set of fears, anxieties and will no doubt bring up insecurities for you. But rest assured this is all natural and this process is essential for opening up your humanity and humility and inviting your readers to share from a deeper connection that some writers would be too afraid or guarded to consider. This vulnerability is what is going to turn your bog-standard writing into wholehearted, relatable, wise story-telling that smashes into the hearts of your readers like a sledge hammer. You may break through their hearts making them look truth in the eye but you will also be the glue that bonds it back together and there you will remain for as long as it beats.

There are millions of books in the marketplace. There are thousands of books published on Amazon, daily. And, along with a killer marketing strategy, you want your book to stand out for its content – and you're not going to make that happen if you're churning out writing that doesn't resonate or connect with your audience.

Your book needs to be authentically YOU. The only way you're going to achieve this is if you allow yourself to be seen... the good, the bad, the funny, and the sad. Readers want to relate to the content they read. Readers want to live that journey through you so they can learn from you. Even in fiction, readers take things away that bring meaning to their lives.

Just like writers should write for purpose – readers will read for meaning. If there's nothing in it for them, if there's no heart they can relate to, if there's no deep and meaningful connection, then you may as well not bother. If the writing doesn't validate the time spent reading your book, they'll move on until they find another one that does. So, getting it right is crucial.

We are in a time when speaking up and standing out for the right reasons is a sign of courage, and people are beginning to understand that every courageous moment follows a vulnerable one.

Over the following chapters of this book, I will delve deeper into the conscious undertaking of committing to writing from the heart.

You should continue reading this if you are aware of the need to put yourself on the page but are afraid of the response.

You should continue reading this if you think that what you have to say is just the same as everyone else. I'll prove otherwise.

You should continue reading this if you think vulnerability is a weakness and should be hidden from your writing.

You should continue reading this if you yearn to write a book about your experience but are struggling to find value in what you have to offer.

You should continue reading this if you understand that the connection between writer and reader comes from a place of wholeheartedness, and you want to learn how to realise this, and increase your ability to connect with your audience.

If you're considering writing a book, which I anticipate you are because you're still reading, learning to write with technical flare is good, but learning to write with your whole heart is better.

I can't wait for you to get stuck in and learn how to create a conversation that stirs up action, ignites hearts across the world and creates connections where there were none. After all, isn't that what happens when you do something with all your heart?

Respectfully your guide,

Cheryl x

Cheryl Hart

Chapter 1
What is Wholehearted Writing?

*"Wholeheartedness. There are many tenets of wholeheartedness, but at its very core is vulnerability and worthiness; facing uncertainty exposure, and
emotional risk, and knowing that I am enough."*

Brene Brown

Firstly, let me tell you a secret. When I began to write from a place of wholeheartedness it scared the crap out of me. So much so that I didn't want to show anyone what I'd written. Sound familiar? This wasn't just because I was concerned of how my writing would be judged. It was because I'd laid my soul bare. My heart's secrets were now in written form.

All those thoughts that never left my mouth were

now pouring onto the blank page in the same way a fallen bottle of red wine makes contact with an otherwise immaculately clean carpet. It is one of the most unsettling things you can do, and once someone reads what you've written, in the same way as someone might look at red wine as it melts into that cream carpet... you wonder... will I ever get that stain out?

We've always been told from a professional point of view that if it's in writing, it can't be unwritten. It's set in stone. Binding. So what does that say for wholehearted writing? If you put your whole heart onto the page and create a literary piece and someone doesn't like it, and you already know you can't take it back because it's out there, either digitally, in print, or audio... it begs the question, if you were to be so open and honest and authentic, wouldn't that jeopardize your perceived worth and what you're trying to accomplish?

Before I answer this, I want you to know that we as people, let alone writers, will never please everyone. *You will never please everyone.* Everyone will never please you. And you wouldn't expect them to. Just to know this, to know and feel okay that you understand that 'everyone' will never please us all at the same time, makes the idea of you not pleasing everyone else a little easier to grasp. And that's okay. Because you're not here to please everyone. If you were then you would be at the mercy of others to make you happy, and hopefully, you have learned that happiness comes from within and is completely within your control. You have the right to accept this now, or perhaps you will accept it easier after a little more experience, or maybe you can admire the idea from a far-off place of doubt and uncertainty and look to a more secure existence, where those who have accepted they cannot please everyone reside, and who are doing their thing regardless.

When you make peace with this sentiment, you begin to segment your audience. You are not writing for every single human in the world for them all to read at the same moment and for them all to go away with the same understanding. As much as we are created with heart and soul, we are all different, going through different experiences, feeling different emotions at different times in our lives. What may be meaningful to one person, may be irrelevant to another. But that doesn't mean that what you have written is irrelevant or de-valued. It means that you need to know your audience. You may choose your audience, but you can't control who reads your work. Those that don't fall into your target readership may still read your work. They may decide to read it but don't relate to its content. If someone doesn't relate, their views may differ from those who do connect with it in the way you intended. It doesn't mean your writing is bad – but what it does present to you is a keen eye for a targeted audience, and a keen ear for feedback from the readers you wrote it for.

When you write for your reader, it should be as if you are writing to them personally, taking them in, drawing their attention so that they feel that the attention of your story is on them. When someone doesn't relate, how can it possibly have the same effect? It can't. You can't ask a person who hasn't been in a relationship to understand the trappings of a vicious, heart-breaking divorce.

It could be that those who pick your book up by accident might not like it at the time, but those same readers may replay your words later in life. Then and only then will the time be right. They may choose to read it again, and like magic, the light turns on and they connect with your words and your story and your heart, and they carry away a powerful message of purpose and the possibility of sparking transformation.

Your audience grows, reshapes, evolves. It is a never-ending evolution of people coming and going as they grow and shift into different forms of themselves.

So, my answer to the question put to you earlier is NO. Wholehearted writing is not a recipe for professional suicide. In fact, I believe it's essential for a successful author to make a lasting connection with the reader through butterfly writing that imparts wisdom and truth.

Even writers of fiction put their whole hearts into their writing. They create fantasy worlds and characters and make them mouth pieces for what the author thinks the world needs less of, or more of, or just simply wants to show the reader that there's hope in getting what their heart desires. Fiction, whilst it might be make-believe-escapism, is in fact largely based on fact and the lives and experiences around us. It's a lot easier to use characters to express your thoughts and opinions, your fears and insecurities, your pride and even your judgement of others and blame it all on the characters of your imagination.

There is a literary term called 'The Death of the Author' which questions where the book begins and the author ends – and if the author ever really leaves the pages of what they're writing.

You could say hiding behind fiction is an illusion. We still see the author. We still hear them. We still feel their joy, their sadness, their passion and their pain. If you choose to write fiction or non-fiction, writing from the heart should still be your number one place to start.

A writer needs to draw from something deep from the well of life. In many cases it will be your life or from the lives and relationships around you. You can draw on their emotion, their feelings, their fears. Tuning into insecurities and fears and the things that stop you or them from taking action, or achieving what your heart desires most in the world, is the very stuff that your reader will relate to. Wholeheartedly.

We are all akin to struggle, fear and scarcity. We are all akin to love, belonging and the ebb and flow of life. Books connect us as individual readers with these aspects of life. They reach for us and say, 'You're not alone in this.'

Our stories form part of the human condition

in that we must connect. Most of us thrive on human connection. We thrive on learning and growing and trying new things. Some of you are afraid to voice opinion, are afraid to be heard as anything away from the chorus of everyone else; or are afraid to say what you really hope for as you fear that you might be seen as lonely, unlovable, weak, weird, or something else. And as much as you may want to take the plunge and dive right in and wait for the change in the way people see you, we are also desperately trying to avoid change, because change leads us into fear and scarcity, and this makes us reach back into familiar territory where we know we are safe.

This brings us neatly back to Wholehearted Writing and why we need more of it within the pages of the books we read. To fully connect with a reader and the world around you, whether it be in the realms of fiction or non-fiction. Whether you're writing a character into a fantasy novel or are producing a HOW TO GUIDE on the over 50s dating scene – you must first establish that, in order for your book to be different, in order for your story to create impact, you must first be willing to open up your heart, to strip away the layers that protect you, and become willing to be seen. As you go through this process, you may uncover aspects of yourself or your behaviours and responses to life that surprise you. You have to be prepared to be exposed and trust that your audience will welcome you warmly. When it's the right audience, they will.

When I finally showed my first piece of Wholehearted Writing to a trusted someone, I was stiff with fear. It quickly passed as I learnt the impact it made. I could see her shoulders relax. I noticed her breathing smooth out. She got it.

She got me. Her final comment I threw away because I felt confused. As she handed the paper back to me, she asked if the story was about her. I realised over a decade later, having read someone else's feedback on a course I'd written, that when someone asks if you'd written the story about them, it's not an accusation. It's a compliment. What I had managed to do, in both this article and this memoir course, was write in a way that made the reader feel like I was telling their story and was talking directly to them. These readers felt so connected to my wholehearted writing that they couldn't help but relate and feel that my heart was the same as theirs. The way in which we process such a moment differs, but the essence of both were that wholehearted writing, writing from that place of unguarded freedom, is when a reader and writer connect in the most powerful way. We are one. We are the same. Our heart's want the same things. Our heart's feel the same way. Nothing is shameful or embarrassing or off limits.

Wholehearted Writing is a way of you reaching out, in blind faith I might add, hoping that someone also has the same concealed thoughts as you, and that someone needs to read your words so that they become less alone and more connected.

Wholehearted Writing is opening up your heart and using your blood as ink. Wholehearted Writing is being courageous, making yourself vulnerable, so that you can show your strength.

What does Wholehearted Writing Mean? Wholehearted Writing shows that you're not afraid to get your hands dirty for the greater good, and not just your own good. It means that for the good of others, you are willing to be honest and expose your most vulnerable pain points. As a wholehearted writer, a Butterfly Writer in the making, you are committing to being authentic. You are stepping forward into the light and not hiding behind falsehoods and ego.

Ask yourself 'When was the last time a book really spoke to me?' and 'When did I feel that connection?'

I can bet that when you began reading that book whether it be non-fiction or fiction that something spoke to you from the very beginning. Personally speaking, if a book doesn't draw me in within two sentences, I put it back.

The first sentence is its first chance. The second sentence is its last. This may sound harsh, but there are soooo many books out there that there is no point wasting your time on a book that feels like a challenge, and I'm not talking about the type of book that should be a challenge to stretch the mind. I'm talking about a narrative that grabs you by the shoulders and pulls you in with just a few words.

We're all so busy needing different things at different times. Books should be purposeful. They serve different meanings to us at different times in our lives. So we must all read with purpose. Admittedly, this can also be for pleasure or escapism. Whatever the reason you read, as long as that narrative talks to you like you're opening a letter from a friend, it will have purpose to fulfil in your life. You should feel that close to it from the very beginning. This is how you know that you've connected with it and the book in your hands holds meaning for you.

I find now that reading material jumps out at me. When it jumps, I catch it. If it falls short, it goes back on the shelf. This is not to say that a book that falls short for me will do the same for others. I mentioned this earlier. What works for one does not necessarily mean it will work for the person standing next to them, because everyone's journey is unique.

I like to think that a book comes along at the right time, for the right purpose. So, when a book jumps, I pay attention. Every single time.

I can't afford to miss anything that might be important that will give me what I need to move forward in my life. This is what you should hold when you think of the people who might read your book. It is for them. It has purpose. It will find them.

Books to me are subliminal messages. Which is why I believe in Wholehearted Writing. For a book to be that powerful, it needs to exude soul, reason, validation and relate to me on a level that goes way beyond the superficial. The heart of the book needs to connect with my heart. How you recognise this is through the energy you feel when you begin to read. There is no other way of explaining it. If it draws you like a magnet – read it.

Books are conversation starters. Books are discussion topics. Books have the power to create change. Books give voices to the voiceless. Books can alter a person's perception and support a happier existence.

You have the power to do all this with your book. You have the power to connect to a reader like no one else has. You have the power to start a conversation which may change the direction of someone's life if you write from the heart. Isn't that worth writing with wholeheartedness, so that you're giving the same value into the writing as the reader is giving to the words you write?

Let me end this chapter with one final note. Your book may not be for everyone, but it may be the spark of transformation for many. Be brave. Be courageous. Be vulnerable. And watch the beautiful fear and scarcity drift away and be replaced with connection and belonging.

Wholehearted Writing Practice

Often, it is the things we least want to write about that we really should be writing about.

Consider a challenging time in your life (whether this is part of the book you plan or not) and write out the feelings that this moment brings about.

You may only need to write a sentence, as a sentence can say a thousand words, or you can write a paragraph or more. It is entirely up to you.

Once you have written as directed, I want you to then read it back, aloud. Really hear the words. This is how a reader will read them.

Rest assured that should you ever choose to show this piece to anyone, make sure it is to a trusted someone that understands you, relates to you and can resonate with you. This makes all the difference at these early stages whilst your confidence is building and you're finding your voice and your audience.

Affirmations for Wholehearted Writing

I set my heart free and trust that it will be safe.

My heart holds truth, and that truth is safe with my reader.

I can write from the heart. My heart is safe.

My writing is my soul. It deserves to be free.

When I write from the heart, I connect wholeheartedly with others like me.

I am a wholehearted writer. I am a butterfly writer.

Butterfly Writer

Cheryl Hart

Chapter 2
The Key Principles of Wholehearted Writing

"Don't dance around the perimeter of the person you want to be. Dive deeply and fully into it."

Gabrielle Bernstein

Now you know that the essence of Wholehearted Writing is being brave enough to write what's in your heart, you can take the next step into understanding its key principles. Let's look at this in a simplistic way. There are three principles to Wholehearted Writing:

1. Vulnerability
2. Courage
3. Connection

These three principles form a cyclical behaviour. Vulnerability leads to courage and courage through vulnerability leads to connecting with others. This cycle doesn't just work with writing, it works within any medium whether that be talking, painting, acting, dancing, or simply living life. If we don't step out of our comfort zone, then we never see what greatness we can achieve. Whatever way you choose to express vulnerability you will have an effect on the observer, in that they will be able to see your courage shine through the action you take.

For the purpose of this book (and what you plan to write) we will focus on being vulnerable in your writing. We will explore how presenting yourself as vulnerable takes courage, and in turn, how such vulnerability and courage leads to strong connections with readers. Note, this is not just any connection. This is the greatly coveted lasting connection between a writer and a reader. To write and to be understood is a gift, but only a gift that can be achieved through honesty, a sense of self and authentic reflection.

Vulnerability

As I mentioned earlier, allowing yourself to be vulnerable, or in this case presenting yourself as vulnerable, is one of the hardest things to do. This method is asking you to pour yourself onto the page. It asks for you to unlock what could be the darkest parts of you and shine a light on them for all to see.

This, no doubt, may be challenging enough for you alone to witness. It may be difficult for you to see the words as they show up on the page. It might be painful and uncomfortable. You may discover aspects of yourself or your journey that you weren't aware of and weren't prepared to realise.

You see, when you write, when you write from the heart freely, unguarded and unashamed, it's as if those words come from another place in your soul. A place that perhaps guards you when you're weak and filters aspects of your journey so that you can get through whatever challenges stand before you. This place could be described as evangelical almost – like the gatekeeper that tells us only what we need to know when we need to know it.

However, after a time, when in post-reflection of events, the protective arms of this place bestow wisdom upon us, as if the oracle of our path is sitting waiting to be prompted to share what we have learnt.

At times of such reflection or even at times amidst great challenges, this place is a source of knowledge and power and even sanctuary. Without digressing too much into this phenomenon of the mind, it is only right that you're aware that you have the tools within you that help you to work out how events occur, how they affect you individually and even how they affect others. This wisdom, if you choose to see it, becomes powerful in the sense that you can heal or grow with the knowledge that you have learnt something valuable along the way. When we write from the heart with unguarded freedom, we allow our truth to be revealed, and that truth when you first write it down might be the first time you become aware of it. This is the power of writing.

To ask yourself questions and allow the answers to form on a page is quite an extraordinary practice to undertake. This could be the very first step in learning to write from the heart. To ask your heart what it wants or how it feels could be the introduction you need to access this place of truth. When the answers are revealed, there comes a point when you take ownership of those feelings and the vulnerability within. This in itself is courage. To own a feeling of vulnerability, acknowledgement is the first step in overcoming it.

Of course, there will be self-doubt when you're at the stage of handing over your vulnerabilities for other people to read. Will others understand? Can others empathise? Will anyone relate? Along with the self-doubt that towers over you in sharing your story, there will be an element of whether to trust that your readers will accept you.

We have grown into this world with the idea that we must be strong, that we must show only strength. We have been pre-conditioned with ideals of what we are supposed to look like, how we should dress, the correct way to open a conversation, to be polite, to not worry others unnecessarily.

The result of this pre-conditioning and conformity is that we are scared to say how we really feel. We may have climbed a mountain, we may have built a successful business from nothing, we may even have raised six kids single-handedly through independent parenting. The story can be as foreign to someone as an alien landing or as familiar as looking upon their own back garden. The way you tell that story defines the way you connect it to the hearts of readers.

There are two ways a story can be told.

Version one might look something like this:

"I climbed that mountain. Mount Everest was my goal and I kicked its ass!"

Version two might look something like this:

"It was just me and that mountain for a long time. There were moments I thought I might never make it down. I lost myself for a while up there. My mind went into a really dark place."

Would you be more interested in the story told in version one or the story told in version two? Does version one sound as authentic as version two? Finally, do you think a raw, honest account of what really happened up that mountain will attract more positive attention than version one's gloating?

Hopefully, the majority (if not all) of you will conclude that there is strength in opening up about vulnerability. For the few that might think version one is better, I hope in time you will come to see the heart in version two and how that heart has power. Afterall, we are only human, and most of us prefer not to be measured against unrealistic caricatures that aren't willing to reveal their insecurities.

The one extra element we get from a story that

spills vulnerability onto the pages of a book is hope. There could be a thousand people wanting to make that climb up the mountain, but can't because they are surrounded by notions of superhuman strength, stamina and mental ability. But by reading about the vulnerability of a person's journey, and how they almost came to fail on several occasions; how they almost lost themselves in doing so, this story becomes inspirational and reachable and authentic. The reader begins to see not a superhuman – but an average person – just like them. When readers see that the seemingly amazing authors of success stories are every inch as vulnerable as themselves, it's a natural next step for that reader to think, 'That could be me.'

This is the essence of vulnerability. If you let your readers in beneath that shield of strength that protects you from the outer world, you won't be turned away for being weak. You'll be embraced for showing how hard you fell at times, and how you picked yourself back up and continued to climb in the face of that fear, self-doubt and uncertainty.

It may seem absurd to believe that your audience needs to feel the elements that made you feel like you couldn't carry on. But it's absolutely true. Including this detail is not you being a victim – it's about you being real. Readers will not only relate to these moments, they will applaud them, because this is how readers can begin to see themselves in your story. People will want to read your story for a reason.

You may be writing a Business How To Guide, or you may be writing a Single Parent Survival Guide, you could even be writing about your climb up Everest. Regardless of your topic, your readers will fall into two camps; those that want to live vicariously through you, again needing to see what makes you human, and those that will want to learn from your experience to encourage and enhance their own journey in the same or similar event.

Your vulnerability teaches others that it's okay to get scared. It's okay to mess up. And it's okay to get things wrong. Because vulnerability is no test of character. The true test is shown in how you get back up and push on through regardless. These are the facts that will be measured and treasured.

Courage

When you make space for vulnerability you automatically create a space for courage. In the words of Brene Brown, 'the two co-exist'.

People often feel shame when they're vulnerable and the last thing anyone wants to do is expose that shame for all the world to see. So, we have to look at vulnerability through a different lens. We have to see the direct link between vulnerability and courage, and once we do, we come to see presenting that vulnerability as a courageous act.

We need to relate to what we read for it to make a significant impact in our lives. There's always an opportunity to see courage within a vulnerable situation. Think back to all the superhero movies of our lifetime: Superman, Batman, The Avengers. These superhuman characters don't appear at times of peace, calm and tranquillity. They appear through moments of conflict. These moments make them vulnerable. What they do next makes them courageous. You see, without vulnerability there would be no courage. Sharing your vulnerabilities will make your story strong, and the connection with your reader deeper, more sincere and longer lasting.

Courage allows your reader to see how you got back up, how you fought the odds and how you powered on to the next step. Vulnerability and courage are the two components most likely to result in making a connection that goes way beyond the, 'Look at me! I did this because I'm awesome!' statement. You may hold a person's attention for a short while with this message, but be prepared to lose it again after a matter of minutes.

Connection

Okay, I'm hoping that by now you understand that there's strength in revealing your vulnerabilities as well as your successes. The connection between vulnerability and courage allows others to perceive you as having felt fear, doubt, and faced challenges, just like every other person on this planet. And this is what's going to make you relatable.

Relatability is paramount when it comes to the writer and reader relationship and the story in between. Whether you tell it as a work of fact or a work of fiction, the characters or real-life people that you're portraying need to be identified with. They need to be made of flesh, muscle, bone and blood because your characters and your writing need to be able to bleed realism. They need to be filled with the emotional capacity of the reader. These characters need to be placed in situations where emotions run high and risk is great.

Connection is all about being with like-minded people. If you're writing this book for yourself (at least at first), then connection between your heart and your writing will be less scary. You will write. You will read it. The words when realised may sting and the reality of your words on the page may be uncomfortable. When writing for yourself you get to close the book and put what you've written away in the peace that no one else will read it. A secret between you and the pages it's written on. Whilst this in itself is recommended for anyone who wants to write, and who wants to practice wholehearted writing, at some point, you may want to branch out and write for a bigger readership.

When this time comes, you should know that your readership should be a community of people who you can relate to and who can relate to you.

You could be writing a book empowering women

to make better choices for themselves. Your audience could be women who have trouble putting themselves first, in saying NO, or who feel tied to decisions and commitments that harbour limitations for themselves.

You will know your audience well because you are your audience. You've been there. You've made hard decisions and difficult choices to free yourself. And here you are, post reflection of the events that led you here, able to see how you've evolved into something you never imagined possible. You're telling your story, providing guidance for those people who are ready to take the same steps you did. Your stories may not be identical, but the essence of needing to take your power back into your own hands, will be mirrored through the needs of your reader.

This is exactly where you want your readers to be. You want them first to relate with the vulnerability of your story, and next to be eating out of the palm of your hand, learning what they need to know, so they can follow in your footsteps, whether vicariously or in reality.

When you write from the heart you take a risk. That risk makes you vulnerable. But if you write with purpose and with the intention of reaching an intended reader, that vulnerability has the opportunity to be a story of courage and hope for others.

When a reader is connected, they will want to stay committed to you. This means that they'll read your book. They'll stay with your story until the very last page. They may even recommend it to a friend, or ten! They'll put your advice into action and they'll seek out more books that you've written. This is not only bonding a connection between writer and reader, it's the start of building a community of like-minded people who value what you have to share.

You'll have a lasting connection, and the one thing you can thank for that, is your courage to make yourself vulnerable in your writing to connect with your audience on a deeper and more authentic level, so they in turn see themselves in you.

Wholehearted Writing Practice

I want you to take one moment of vulnerability. Write it down. Then I want you to write down what you did in that vulnerable moment to get back to a place of safety. This could be discovering your bank account is on zero and your rent needs paying and you just received an eviction notice. Your next step could be asking for help. Asking for help is a sign of courage. Creating an awareness in that space is courage. Not running away and looking the truth in the eye is courage.

It doesn't have to be a heroic display of vulnerability and courage that might be worthy of a superhero movie. It just needs to be real. The most vulnerable moments are our everyday moments. So be truthful, and remember to be kind to yourself, because vulnerability and courage is a strength intertwined, and to demonstrate both in your writing, will reward you with connection.

Affirmations to Encourage Connection

It's okay for me to show vulnerability.

My heart holds truth, and that truth is what will resonate with my reader.

When I write from my soul, I am understood.

To share vulnerability is courage.

I am courageous.

Vulnerability and courage lead to valuable connection.

Cheryl Hart

Chapter 3
Every Writer's Worst Enemy

"The Worst enemy to creativity is self-doubt."
Sylvia Plath

When I used to think of a writer, I would associate them with intellect, reason, education, purpose, a strong voice, opinion, authority and a Godly presence that was unquestionable.

I looked upon a writer as someone who stood out from the crowd with their superior knowledge of language, their perfectly balanced way with syntax, and their ability to create a written work that was not covered in red pen after marking (much like my own work throughout my school years). I imagined such authors to be proficient students (unlike the fifteen-year-old version of me), eager to learn, academia at their heart with an unfaltering respect from their teachers and other authoritarian figures.

I had formed a stereotype with this set of characteristics. They began to fill my idea of the type of person that would be allowed to write. That permission of authoritarian figures that were authors, publishers, teachers and other professionals would seek out well-educated, well-mannered writers and licence them with the permission of becoming an author. These debut authors would become a voice that the world would take seriously. Their opinion would be based on reason and fact and after spending years of writing in journals and being at the top of their game, they would articulate themselves with the same proficiency as an English Professor, or at least, they could if they chose to.

I thought that these 'writers' were born into an advanced vocabulary and an authoritarian sense of respect and general social standing. I imagined they learnt all they could at an early age, were ranked top of the league and then, and only then, subject to ticking off an extensive list of societal stature and academic achievement, this would catapult them into the nether regions of the future Gods and Goddesses of literature. Untouchable, unreachable, and dare I say it, unachievable for many, many others.

Yet, it's worth mentioning that some writers lack emotive intelligence, and the emotional intelligence that you pick up through living out your experiences. It's this that can be more powerful than the writing techniques you can learn in college. Emotional intelligence is defined to have five characteristics: self-awareness, self-regulation, motivation, empathy and social skills. When a high level of emotional intelligence exists in a person, discovering the wisdom in the events that occur in life will be easier to process, and therefore, that intelligence will be available to pass on. These experiences, if learnt from and shared with heart, can transform you into an author that connects deeply with your wisdom and your audience.

My idealistic notion of a writer, all my praise and worship of such authors of my childhood, adolescence and my young adulthood was completely unfounded. All this idealism did for me was hold me back. I didn't realise that an author was just a person. That's right. Every author whether it be Stephen King, Marianne Keyes or Gabrielle Bernstein is just an everyday human being writing from the heart.

They are not super-human. They feel vulnerability

just as easily as you and I. It's what makes them great writers because they know how to write from the heart. The heart of love. The heart of fear. What also makes them great writers is their dedication and commitment to the craft and understanding their audience. Writing is a craft. You will always be reaching to perfect it. You will never hit the limit of being the best at your game because with writing there are no limitations, and because language continues to evolve, and the way we converse continues to adapt and change and move with the times, writing will always be a shapeshifter recognising the need for change and the requirement to move with social culture and reader expectations.

Joe Moran, a teacher of university students and author of *First You Write a Sentence*, sets out to clear the misconception that writing a sentence is easy. He goes on to say that it takes a lifetime 'to perfect' this craft. There is no age in which you become expert, as Moran suggests, you just keep your attention on the words in front of you, their meaning and how they balance and hang together as one sentence.

He goes on to suggest, and I can vouch for him here that, even at university level, students struggle with writing a fully formed sentence. So much so, that he tells of an assignment set by Wendell Berry, a teacher of English at the University of Kentucky in the 1980s, who set his graduate students this assignment: Write a single sentence.

He goes on to explain the reasons for this assignment were that English Professors were used to being presented with the language of youth; fragmented sentences, and ideas that don't get started. I can honestly say that during my time at university, I was accused of this same misuse of language from my lecturers more often than I liked. They were quick to pull me up on fragmented sentences that I'd pulled in from my creative writing techniques (for creative writing they can be very useful to highlight things you want the reader to notice), and half-baked ideas that hadn't been explored enough before I'd gone on to the next.

During my time writing advertising copy, fragmented sentences drew attention to a product or a consumer need. Fragmented sentences have their place in written language. We see them all the time when reading promotional material. So, it stands to reason that we might adopt a fragmented sentence here and there to make a point. That said, it wasn't the type of syntax a university professor is hoping to read from an english language or literature student. This was me and about every other fellow student in my class. Reasons for the common use of fragmented sentences are in the way we speak, listen and read. We're constantly listening, reading and speaking fragmented sentences because the media is trying to catch our attention, trying to evoke reaction, in the very little airtime they have our attention for. Creative writing techniques work very well in advertising also.

For example: **Selling fast!** is a fragmented sentence. The sentence leads to more questions about what that sentence means. What's selling fast? Where? A full sentence should have more detail so that the reader understands clearly what the subject and purpose of the sentence is.

For example: **The shoes at The Bay are selling fast.**

This simple sentence has more information, and is not fragmented - yet I'm sure you can agree that the fragmented sentence is more arresting for marketing material and creating buzz around a sale.

On a subliminal level, we are absorbing these fragmented sentences and then using them in our own forms of communication.

Another reason for error in sentence structure is the use of word processors. This type of software also offers a helping hand in spelling, grammar and offers suggestions when 'it thinks' you got it wrong. Note, 'it' doesn't always get it right either.

Now, if you consider my first thought about my ideology of a writer and juxtapose it with Wendell Berry's assignment to his English class, hopefully, you can join me in appreciating that even English under-graduates get it wrong. Perhaps another reason for this, as Berry suggests, is due to the speed in which these word processors allow our thoughts to become words on the page. It is suggested that speed has taken over careful consideration of the right word for the right sentence.

As with everything, writers new and old need to find the right balance between allowing thoughts to escape and creating meaning in the words we write.

During my time as a writer, I have taken many

knocks. I have got back up on countless occasions, started again, tried something new, or gone back to an old written work and been either horrified or amazed that I had written it. If you're reading this book then you're considering writing a book, or may have already began, or might be on a second draft, or a second book and looking to enrich your craft. If any of these is you, I want you to take on board that writers are not born writers. Just as heroes don't fall out of the sky and save the day, writers don't jump out of the womb and demand a pen and paper.

Writers are everyday people, doing everyday things, experiencing everyday hopes and fears, losses and gains.

Anyone can become a writer just like anyone can become a hero. If the opportunity and circumstances are right you can become anything of your choosing. What you do need is passion in your topic, and commitment to your goal. If you have each of these, then you're well on your way to learning the craft and increasing your skill in telling your story and writing your book.

I'm sharing this because there are many misguided pre-conceptions that tell people that you need permission to write a book. The many eye rolls or the 'Who do you think you are?' comments only go to prove my point that i'm not alone in my past idealistic notion of a writer. Of course, it stands to reason, that if I could think it, then many others would be thinking the same thing too. And it's high time this type of thinking stopped because EVERYONE has the authority and permission to write a book and become the author of their story.

The Trouble with the Imposter

When we begin to write we are in fact asking to be perceived as someone who knows. Someone who has been there. Someone who wants to share their story. Someone who can articulate a concept or a theory or a how-to-guide so that others can enjoy, be entertained or follow. I don't think I'm alone in feeling that I needed permission to write a book. I don't think I'm alone in worrying whether critics (professional or personal) might question my choice of language, or consider my plots to be half-hearted mish-mash that they could do better themselves.

Going back to my previous chapter on vulnerability and courage. It takes courage to put yourself on the page, and for all those people that feel able to comment on your work but have no experience in doing the work themselves – they can either pick up a pen and paper and see just how much of them it takes to do this – or they can go ahead and sit back down and talk about something else. People who have no experience in writing a book have no place to comment on yours with negative criticism and judgement.

It takes courage to define your audience. To write JUST for them. To remember that everyone else doesn't matter. It takes courage to listen to the opinions of readers that don't fall into your target audience, because they will have plenty to say, or worse, they become silent whilst trying to dress up their criticism with polite smiles whilst scratching around for something they liked.

The trouble with these types of opinions is that they feed the gremlins within us, and these thoughts can quickly evolve into self-doubt. Self-doubt is the worst enemy of any writer. Once it kicks in, you may find yourself having trouble identifying with the wisdom of what you write, and instead switch to identifying with feelings of the imposter.

This is when you have to (and I mean HAVE TO)

segment all criticism into two groups:

1. Opinions from your audience

2. Opinions from everyone else

Otherwise, you'll end up running from yourself, the work you've written and the writer that you've become, all because of someone's opinion that you shouldn't validate in the first place. You may begin to ask yourself, Who am I to call myself a writer? Who am I to say I have a story to tell that others can benefit from in some way? Why does my experience matter?

Once you go down this road (and we may each traverse this at some point) it takes a while to find your way out, but I can guarantee that when you do, you'll be a stronger writer for it.

Regardless of what you write or who you write for, you are validated as a writer. You do not need to sell a million books on Amazon. You do not need to get a publishing contract with Penguin, and you do not need to be featured on Oprah for your life changing revelation to be validated as worthy. You are a writer just as you are.

Self-Doubt and Negative Self-Talk

Some of you may be writing a book as part of a

larger business strategy. For others this could be the beginning of your business. Whilst another reason could be that you've always wanted to write the story running round your head and finally have committed yourself to writing that book.

I'll warn you now that there will be times that, regardless of your reason and your book's purpose in your life or your business, that self-doubt and negative self-talk will rear their annoying heads.

But don't worry. You have one weapon against them. You're now expecting them. Expectation is your weapon, and when you expect something, you can plan for it.

Self-doubt and negative self-talk will show up at some point. Surprisingly, it might not be when you're in the midst of writing your way into a corner that you're struggling to get out of. It might be when you're at the precipice of a great writing flow. Suddenly a thought crosses your mind and knocks you off your stride.

You could be having the best writing day ever. You may have just signed with a big publisher, or you may have just finished the first draft of your book. The immense pride and celebration that comes with finally having something tangible in front of you brings you joy and gratitude. Everything is going great, right? Then out of nowhere Fear and Scarcity barge through your mind and knock Joy and Gratitude off their stride, leaving them stammering in the background. This is when you need to act quickly and be prepared to catch them before your mind runs wild with all the 'You can't do this', 'Just who do you think you are?' and 'They're going to hate it' messages – which, I might add, are just old messages resurfacing waiting to see if you still think the same as you used to.

When these thoughts run free, they create anxious moments that become stalling. You may begin to reason with the fact that writing this book is earning you zero income right now. That maybe it's a pipe dream that needs squashing or that your time is better spent elsewhere, doing things that other people do that's ordinary, average and understood.

And, if you give it enough thought, all of these things will be right and just might be enough to convince you to throw in the towel. Thoughts can be our own worst enemy.

Put simply, we have to nurture our thoughts. We

have to be aware of them. We have to put in the time to change things that no longer work for us. We have to understand the measure of our immediate responsibilities, the challenges we may face, and keep in mind that this book is an investment. It is costing nothing but your time.

When you consider this, you will either tell yourself that time is too tight, or that time is plentiful (you just might need to take it slower than you first expected and alter your schedule if time is an issue). The key to combatting negative self-talk is to know all the types of negatives that might be thrown at you along your writing journey.

These could be:

- I have no time to build in a writing practice
- I am already working all the time
- I am a doctor (or other profession) not a writer
- People don't expect this from me, therefore I should try to maintain their perception

The list is endless for the reasons to stop writing and discard writing a book from your life. But writing a book doesn't have to take over your life. There are ways to fit it in. It may take time but the beauty of giving yourself longer to write it, is that the content you choose will be well considered and not rushed. I find that my best working practice is to write one chapter a day. Just one. This is not only easier to fit into my life but it also allows my creativity to grow and for my 'attention to detail' to recharge overnight, ready to start a new day and a new chapter.

Please note, that I don't write a chapter of a book every day. Only when I have a book project to work on. So, when I commit, I know I can commit wholeheartedly with the discipline needed to get from chapter to chapter, until I reach the end. And I love seeing the end in sight. Once complete, I allow it to rest for a few weeks, or even months, if it feels right. Then I begin the editing and re-draft process which is soooo much nicer than the structural formation of a first draft.

If you consider writing your book as a temporary project, it will get done and be finished much faster if you commit to a chapter a day. More if you like. This practice will have you writing your book in no time at all and soon enough you'll see the reward of that dedication.

I appreciate that many of you will have full time jobs and writing will be within your leisure time, and yes it will take dedication and commitment. Some people's leisure time may be spent reading, at a bar, hanging with friends or just sitting in front of the television in a bid to wind down from your work hours.

Hopefully, you're at a time in your life when this book that you plan to write is pressing on your to do list, and cutting the time out of that leisure time will be a part of that sacrifice to get that book written. However, if you love to write and you love to escape in your writing, then this could be the nicest part of your day or evening.

Please know that you can be a practiced healer / writer. You can be a teacher / writer. You can be an engineer / writer. It is much more common these days for people's careers to be split across different industries. One that pays the bills and one that brings you joy and success. Whatever your reason for writing this book, don't let go of it. Just because it's not paying you yet doesn't mean that it won't in the future. Make time and commit to writing and know that if writing is bringing you joy, then that joy is feeding your soul, and food for the soul is worth more than its weight in gold. You are worthy to write from the heart and ignite connection with yourself and with others.

Wholehearted Writing Practice

Draw a line down the centre of an A4 piece of paper. On the left write down all the negative thoughts and self-talk that come up for you – ones that may hinder your writing journey. You could even write down other people's comments. Then in the space on the right side, list all the solutions and a positive message to counteract each of these negative thoughts. Once you have written these out, keep them somewhere accessible to drive you through your moments of self-doubt.

For example:

Negative Thought

I am seen as a dentist. People identify with me and my profession. I am a fool to think I can be identified as an author. Who am I kidding?

Positive Thought

I identify as a writer and a dentist. I am allowed to be both. People will identify with me as I identify with myself.

Affirmations for Confidence in Your Writing

I am enough.
What I have to write about is of value to others.
I write in my own words. My words have power.
Writing brings me joy.
I am a writer.
My words have meaning.
My book will hold meaning for others.
I listen to no one but my heart for my heart is where i'm writing from.
There is truth in my writing, therefore there is the potential to earn.
I learn from what I write. As I write I learn new things about myself.
I am entitled to be an author.

Butterfly Writer

Cheryl Hart

Chapter 4
You Are Enough

"So many people bump into our lives for a second and it changes us forever, but they never know it."

Mandy Hale

What we tell ourselves in our heads (over and over again) is that on some level we're inadequate, and in some way, we don't measure up. This message that plays on repeat can be the difference between moving forward into the light and creating something great, and stepping back into the shadow, letting someone else take your place.

The difference is not that one has greater talent, or better supporters, or more followers, or was just lucky to be in the right place at the right time. The difference between the person who steps forward and the person who steps back is how that message is dealt with, because regardless of who you are, that message will be playing over and over. Until you make it stop.

Your Story is Important

Your story is as valid as the air you breathe. Just like oxygen is needed to keep you alive, your story has the potential to rejuvinate the life of another.

There's power in stories. We need stories to connect. We need them to see our world from a different perspective. Stories can act as a window into the soul of a person or the heart of a community. They can teach best practices, emotional empathy, and how to get up after making mistakes. Stories produce the potential for opportunity to be seen and seized. A potential for something other than what the reader might be experiencing in their present moment. In this instance, words have momentous power to activate change.

Your story has the potential to be a life-changing read. It could reach the hands of 10 or it could reach the hands of 10,000 or 10,000,000 readers. Regardless of the readers it reaches, it will never lose its power to capture the hearts of the right people.

Write What You Know

As a guide in writing practice people are told to

write what they know. When you write what you know it comes easy. When you write what you know, you're less likely to need to research elements of the content. However, writing what you know is not just about whether you know business, or yoga practice or a specific moment in history. It's about the connection you have with that subject, the finer details you can research and add for technical accuracy. Yet, the most important and crucial element of writing on your subject is recognising that it connects to your soul and, therefore, the way you write about that subject will come from a deeper place of understanding and emotional connection, which will equal a deeper resonation with your reader. You should ask yourself, what was life like before your experience and what would life have been like without it?

You won't simply be telling your audience about a subject, you'll be showing them how this subject lights up your heart and changed you as a person. Writing as fact or developing a novel, it makes no difference. A reader will still observe character growth and transformation. And regardless of your purpose for writing this book, you will be teaching from a place of passion, love and an energy that makes others want to learn from you or your characters.

A message to be shared through writing what you know is a connection to soul, and that connection can reach another like-minded soul, and that can create a connection for greater things to be achieved by the reader, which may go something like this, 'If she can do it, so can I.' You're selling belief. Asking people to believe in your story and indirectly inviting them to believe in themselves.

Even when you write fiction you must first be aware that human relationships are the focal point of any fictional piece. Whether you write historical fiction or fantasy, human relationships will be the glue that holds it together. Therefore, if you're writing what you know and are inspired by real relationships and real life-events, you're going to produce a narrative that is wholehearted, three dimensional and above all relatable.

The beauty about writing what you know is that sometimes you find out that you know more than you gave yourself credit for. There's a truth to be told that when it comes to teaching others, we also teach ourselves.

In some instances, writing your story could be

the most nourishing and therapeutic writing journey of your life. It could become your emotional therapy, your journey to wisdom and self-awareness, as well as discovering a whole version of yourself that you hadn't recognised before.

The writing process is not always an easy feat, but it is always a worthwhile one. Finding the self within, and to share that self with others, might just be the best worthwhile and wholehearted thing you ever do.

You will Always be Relevant

Your experiences are not less valuable than anyone else's. The relationships that exist in your life are no less validated than another person's. What makes your heart beat is just as important as what makes all the hearts in the world beat.

You see, you and your heart and your story are as important as anyone else's. Period. Don't let that voice inside of you tell you otherwise.

You don't need to be a best-selling author for your story to be deemed relevant. Believing this is the first step to combatting self-doubt. You have the power to quiet the voices in your head with a new message. You have the power to reinforce that message with more new messages. Yes, the old messages will still come through at times, but if you're consistent with the new ones, the old ones will have less room to show up. If you say the new ones often enough, even if you don't believe them at first, eventually, the new messages will start to feel real because you'll begin to feel that they're real and believe in them.

It's so easy to tell ourselves that we don't measure up. But it's just as easy to tell ourselves that we do! Our thoughts are the most powerful things in our bodies. Our thoughts have the power to make us sick. Our thoughts have the power to induce pain. Our thoughts have the power to trick us back into our comfort zone so that we never achieve anything.

But get this, your thoughts also have the power to create joy. They have the power to unlock your potential for greatness. They create curiosity and wellbeing. A single thought can either do a lot of damage or it can create a whole lot of good.

Think of a thought in the same way you think of a ripple effect. One stone thrown into a lake changes that lake forever. Nothing in that lake will return to how it was before that stone entered. The stone has created a ripple effect on the water's surface changing everything those ripples reach, all the way up to the shoreline. Eventually the stone will fall to the bottom of that lake where it will rest. The stone has not only altered the water's surface, it has sunk deep down into the bed of the lake, now resting with all the other stones at the bottom. Another surface forever altered.

Now, think of this stone representing a single thought. Only, what the stone doesn't do within a lake is travel around and pass by each and every element of the lake again and again. This is how thought travels through you. A single thought is carried round the brain, from one neuron to the next, propelled by the most important muscle in the human body. The heart.

In the human body a thought is not just a thought. A thought is a signal to invoke a reaction. Whether you intend it to be or not. Each thought is transmitted from one neuron to another. Like runners in a relay race passing the batton. The neurons in your brain will pass that single thought on to the next neuron, and the next, signalling a reaction within you, before it finally drops into the catalogue of thoughts held by your memory.

Before you know it, this thought has turned into a handful of other negative thoughts, each boosted by the last. Can you imagine the crowd of spectating thoughts whispering resistance to a change in perspective?

To combat self-doubt, first we must understand why we're experiencing self-doubt. We must catch the non-supportive thought that appears, write it down, and when we're aware of this thought, and only when we're aware of it, can we take the power back and begin changing it; shifting perspective and sending it back into our physiology as a nurturing thought that empowers our minds, rather than a negative, limiting one that holds us back.

Combatting Self-Doubt

Self-doubt can come in all forms. It can be channelled from other people who doubt us. It can come from a childhood ideal that only 'authors' should write (like I thought) or it can come from a genuine lack of experience. I'm sure there's a million other reasons for self-doubt, so feel free to add them to this list.

The very first step to combatting self-doubt is to first become aware of that thought, then as mentioned earlier, write that thought down.

Your next step is to re-write that thought. Make a good one. A nourishing one and repeat it as a mantra.

For example: Instead of saying: 'I can't write' Try saying: 'I become a better writer every day.'

Keep them simple, manageable and reachable.

Combatting self-doubt is all about shifting your mindset. Mindset is the number one thing that holds us back. Negative self-talk is a part of that. Yet, mindset is what holds all those thoughts together.

If you tell yourself that you're going to write a book that's going to help inspire or entertain people far and wide, then you're setting the intention to get your book written. Your mindset will be focused, positive and driven.

If you tell yourself that you have a story in you (just like 80% of the world's population) and that one day you're going to write it, then your thought is always 'one day', and for most, 'one day' never comes.

Shifting your mindset will help you not only start to write your book, it will also help you to drive your story into a reality where you're holding your printed manuscript in your hands.

As individuals we happen across the paths of a great sum of people in our lifetime. Without ever knowing or realising, we alter the course of the lives of many. Books have the power to do exactly the same thing.

Your story has the power to create change. Let confidence take control in knowing that someone, somewhere will benefit from reading your story. Make the commitment and embark on making a positive impact with your story because when it comes from the heart, it's received by many others in a wholehearted way.

Wholehearted Writing Practice

In just a few sentences write down the overall message you want your book to say to your reader. Consider the path you've walked, and the path your reader may be walking. Consider the way you wish to connect with your reader and the benefit your story could have on them.

What is the first thing you would say to your reader if you were face to face with them?

Affirmations of Worth

I am worthy.

My story is worthy.

I will connect with readers with a worthy story that will help/heal/teach/inspire/entertain.

Readers deserve to feel worthy too and my story will help them achieve this.

I have no limitations.

I am worthy of this change. I am confident in my worth. I am confident in my story.

The purpose of my story is worthwhile to many.

Butterfly Writer

Cheryl Hart

Chapter 5
Recognising Your Value

"There is nothing to writing. All you do is sit down at a typewriter and bleed."

Earnest Hemingway

Realising the worth in your journey is like finding a treasure chest within yourself. Your journey is a gift. That gift can be passed on to share with others. In order to see the value in your story you must first see it through your reader's eyes.

You must remember that your readers are likely to be behind you on your path. They are unlikely to be at your side at the same place. Those at your side will be looking for a different story, I can assure you.

Focus on the readers that are at the beginning of your journey, or are part way through, or those who have gotten lost and feel stuck. Remembering that it's these people you're speaking to will help you to hold onto the value that your story, your book, and your words has for someone else.

You have the education, the experience and the blood, sweat and words to guide them in where to go next, what to avoid and how to get there faster than you got to where you are. Your story is a gift of transformation from you to them.

Your pain points, the challenging times, and the moments where you made not-so-great-choices become pivotal moments of relatability between you and your readers. A pain point could be a lack of money or nowhere to live, or lack of family support. Pain points can come in all shapes and sizes from the most unlikely places. Often our pain points come from sources we thought we could trust. Your readers will not only thank you for sharing these moments, they will also relate to them, reflect and maybe even find the answers to help ease their own challenges.

Readers need to see themselves in your journey which is why wholehearted story telling - and writing your journey with every inch of your heart is the very best way to secure connections that create new ideas, hope, fulfilment and a plan for a better, faster, and more efficient way for leading your readers to their own goal.

As Earnest Hemingway said, "There is nothing to writing. All you do is sit down at a typewriter and bleed." This is something I teach my students. You can't sit behind your story or your words. You have to be present, exposed and authentic. Your words need to come from that deep place within. The one that pumps the fear, the worry, the horror, the shame, the guilt, the love, the passion, the sex, and the desire. If you aren't prepared to bleed onto the page, then you must be prepared to miss out on connecting with readers in a way that's only possible if you dare to show the truth in your heart.

If you're still sitting on the fence wondering if you have the courage to do this, then think of the strength your story could give to someone else. Sometimes, just knowing that your words have the power to create a positive impact is enough to inspire you to keep sharing. If you were to bump into a friend who shared a similar problem to one you'd already faced, would you keep it to yourself, or would you be happy to share how you tackled it knowing that you're experience may help in some way?

When Readers See Themselves in Your Story

When I read a book, I need to see myself in it.

It doesn't matter if it's fiction or non-fiction, that book will be teaching me something. As a veracious reader I'm aware of this. It's why I read so much, and I never class reading as a waste of time. If I'm reading the right material for me, at the right point in my life, I am certain there will be a message within that story that will somehow contribute to my future choices.

When you begin to write your book you should have already considered your reader avatar. What is a reader avatar? An avatar is a model of the type of person you want to target. A reader avatar is the type of person you think will read your book and enjoy the content. Your book will tell your avatar something about themselves, or their experiences, and your story will leave them feeling understood, encouraged, and inspired.

Do you have an idea of what your reader avatar will look like? If not, I've added some questions to consider to help get you started.

Who is your Reader Avatar?

- Are they male/female/other/all
- How old are they?
- Where do they live?

- Are they rich/poor?
- Are they in love?
- Are they heartbroken?
- Are they in good health or are they sick?
- Do they have a life changing condition?
- Do they have children?
- Do they have pets?
- Do they have a husband or wife?
- Are they in a happy, fulfilling relationship?
- Are they unhappily married?
- Are they in danger?
- Do they over eat?
- Do they harm themselves or others?
- Are they excited by weird people or are they afraid of anyone unusual?
- Do they like sex or do they think it's a sin?
- Are they looking for escape?
- Do they hate their job?
- Do they hate their life?

- What do they read?
- What do they look for in a book?

Creating your reader avatar is as important as creating your characters for your book. The two go hand in hand. They should fit together like a hand in a glove. What one seeks (the reader) the other will give (the book). Identifying your audience and what they're looking for right now is key to you finding the worth in your story and holding onto your value and getting that book written.

Wholehearted writing is a method used to hook the right readers – but first you have to identify the right readers to make sure that the writing and the reader connect. This will also give you more confidence in writing from the heart in knowing that your reader will understand what it is you're saying.

Consider your reader avatar like a section on a business plan. You can research the demand in the reader marketplace to find out how big your audience is.

For example: If you're writing fact or fiction with a theme on mental health for men you only need to turn on the television or radio or open a magazine to get a quick picture that this is a hot topic. A little more digging and you can locate national statistics, and charitable organisation data that help you understand the gravity of this issue. In the UK, it's a well-known fact that men think they need to be strong, therefore talking about mental health whether that be depression or something else is a topic that some avoid.

It's all well and good saying there's a market for your book (which I'm sure there is) but if you're looking for investment to publish your book, then it's a valid use of your time to find out the need and purpose of your story beforehand, and build your findings into your query letter to a publisher further down the line.

A book needs a good launch strategy. The more fuel you can gather around its purpose, the greater success you're going to have in reaching the right people.

Regardless of what you're writing, there'll be a platform that will tell you how much demand there is for a story like yours. Firstly, there are social media groups. Facebook seems a popular platform for groups, and Instagram, is well know for its inspiration and positivity. As mentioned earlier you can approach charities and professional organisations to gather as much information as possible so that your book is as helpful and as authentic and current as it can be.

Requesting access to join social media groups is a brilliant way for you to scope demand for your story, connect with people and receive their stories. As well as social media groups, there is also reading platforms such as Good Reads and Bookbub. Good Reads and Bookbub are useful as you can see what people are reading, what they want more of and what they don't want.

My recommendation would be to join as many groups (social or otherwise) connected to the theme/s within your story, and immerse yourself within the communities that mirror these themes. Learn as much as you can. This will not only produce another level of understanding, it will also be useful as research, as well as gathering data on the importance of completing your book and providing a source of assistance for others.

It makes no difference if you head down the factual route or the fictional one. It's all relevant. Everyone has different needs and wants, just like we have different ideas of what can or can't help us in our lives. Some readers may be less direct and look for a fictional story that they can see themselves in, so they don't feel so alone. Other readers may look for a more direct approach, wanting to look themselves straight in the eye and figure out their next step through a self-improvement book or a memoir.

That doesn't mean to say that one works better than the other. If you're uncertain of which direction to go in start writing out a few lines and see how it begins to form on the page. Does it feel like you can write a whole fiction novel around a selection of themes that drive the purpose of the book, or do you feel you want to just write it as it happened, reflecting back, using your story as inspiration in its purest form?

The best way to decide is to begin writing and see which path your heart chooses. There is value in your story - now try connecting your experience to your reader pain points. This is where value becomes evident.

Wholehearted Writing Practice

Using the reading avatar list above as a guide point, create an avatar of your ideal reader. You don't have to use the list extensively. You may already know who your reader is. Write down their pain points and next to these items on the list – write down an aspect of your story that addresses these points and serves a purpose to your reader.

Affirmations for Value

I find value in understanding who my reader is.

I value the reader's needs.

I am focused on identifying my reader's needs and writing my book to fulfill those needs.

My reader values what I have to share.

My reader will connect with the value of my story, as much as I connect with the value in writing it.

Chapter 6
Wholehearted Reading

"I kept always two books in my pocket, one to read, one to write."

Robert Louis Stevenson

Authors, aspiring authors and writers of everything, even writers of the soul, who only write for themselves within the pages of their journal should read. You should read what makes your heart sing. You should read books that inspire you and put questions to you. There is light reading, and then there is reading with purpose. The books that capture your attention from the first sentence is what you should be reading. The books that make you want to know what happens next, no matter what, are what you should stick with. Books that make you want to write a book or feel like you can write are the books you should pay attention to. In some way or other all of these books will be guideposts for you to learn from and be inspired through. Whenever you feel that tug of discontent in your writing ability go back to these books and see what it is that compelled you to keep reading them. Let your heart and soul be your guide to the type of book you want and need to read.

Every book has a narrative, a storyteller, a voice. This voice can be first person, third person or even second person. It can be sincere, friendly, helpful, wistful or even unreliable at times. Perhaps without your knowledge, when reading a book, you put your trust in the narrator. You read the words that line the pages and a voice appears in your head. Yes, it sounds a lot like your voice, but the language, syntax and story give it its own character, and you might begin to love that voice and want more of it. Whilst we revisit finding your writing voice more in the next chapter, it's important for you to understand that within the context of this chapter and the context of the books you choose to read, that this voice I speak of, the narrator of the story, is with you from the moment you open the book to the moment you finish it. And if the voice is particularly strong, it will have the power to call you back time after time. You see, it's not just the story that compels you to read but the energy with which it's written through its narrative.

Reading should be your number one go-to source of research and reference. Firstly, begin with all the books you've ever loved. Read through them again and try to pinpoint what it is that makes you love them. Secondly, stimulate your writer senses with new material, trying everything you can get your hands on or that fall in your way by accident, to see if they hold anything meaningful for you. Reading books has the power to open a channel for you to escape into worlds separate from your own, even if you're reading non-fiction, someone else's life may be what you want for yourself, and so, this too would be another world entirely to the one you currently reside in. Reach into these books. Understand how the book is giving you what you need and make a note of these points.

Sometimes all we need is what's right in front of us, and sometimes that comes in the shape of a book we've had for all eternity. It's often the case that we don't need to look that far to see where and how we're guided. Which is why it's important to keep your eyes and heart open to everything that feels good when you read it, or when you see it.

When a book is written in a way you understand wholeheartedly, it has the power to squeeze your heart 'til it stings or 'til it sings. You may come across books that use imagery that speak to you in a profound way. It doesn't have to be over-complicated literary prose. You just needs to take the context of what is written and create the simplest form of imagery possible so that every reader will understand the picture presented. This is done effectively when you use imagery that readers will be familiar with.

The way to connect to your reader is not just through the story you tell but in the way you tell it. As a writer, you are reminded at times to show readers, not simply tell them.

The same can be said for anything that we embark on in life. When we are shown how to do something for the first time, we are given a picture or a demonstration to work from. As writers, much of what we deliver to readers is a lesson, and a lesson must undergo a process of understanding; pulled back into steps, given elements of relatability and slowed down for the participant to process.

Writers have many tools at their disposal for this. One of the key tools writers use is imagery. We create a picture in the readers mind which is relatable. We may use a simile such as 'like bees to honey' or we may use a metaphor such as 'My mother is the wind at my back'. Simile and metaphor are your power tools when it comes to readers understanding the image you have in your head to convey an emotion or picture of some sort. The image will not only appear in the reader's mind, depending on the context, it can also be felt in their heart.

Simile is a literary term for when something is compared to something else. For example: Jazmine was as sly as a fox. This sentence uses a simile when the person is compared to the fox's character. The reader is given direction in how to think of Jazmine and not to trust her based on the image they now have of Jazmine juxtaposed with the sly fox. When using simile, the words 'like' or 'as' will often be found as one subject is compared to the other.

Metaphor is another literary term for when one thing is described as something entirely different. For example: 'My mother is the wind at my back' is a metaphor for a driving force pushing you to go further. In the example above, this metaphor describes the mother as being the driving force, but uses the element of wind to show that the mother's encouragement and love follows the subject wherever they go. The subject of wind is being compared to the subject of a mother's encouragement: all encompassing, never faltering, ever-present.

Every book we read provides a collection of images that shows us what the reader wants us to see, and the imagery used should be in keeping with the context of the story, the character, and be easily accessible and relatable to the reader.

Here's another example:

David Mitchell, author of *The Bone Clocks*, begins his story with the narrative of a fifteen-year-old girl experiencing her first heartbreak. We've all been there at some time or other, yet at fifteen the ache is so sweet and the pain so innocent and naive that the author chooses not to just tell the pain, but to show it through metaphor. An image of what her heart and soul look like as she discovers her inappropriately older boyfriend in bed with her best friend is conveyed. As the character leaves the scene emotionally wounded, Mitchell compares her broken heart to 'a clubbed baby seal,' giving the reader a taste of that pain with an image of something that is fragile and vulnerable.

Making that connection between the reader, the book's characters and the story as it unravelled was paramount for Mitchel to identify the best imagery that would sum up the emotional onslaught that readers could relate to. He didn't need to elaborate or dress it up in any other way – those five words say so much more than rows and rows of telling the reader how the character felt.

When I'm writing a book, I rarely do it on my own. What do I mean by this? Well, just like Robert Louis Stevenson, I too have two books on the go at this time. One that I'm writing and one that I'm reading. I would go as far to say that the book I will be reading at the time will be inspiring me from a narrative point of view, a tone of voice or just the way in which it makes me feel. I read only one book whilst I'm writing. It keeps me clear and gives my writing clarity and focus. Read the wrong type of book whilst you're writing, and you could find yourself going down a track you hadn't planned for, because books influence us and they influence how and why we write.

Keeping the right one at hand is very important.

If you haven't tried reading and writing in parallel to one another and would like to see where the influence takes you, make sure you choose a book that speaks your language, is of the same mindset as you and what you're writing, and that it connects with you deeply. The energy of this book should match the energy in which you want to write with.

The imagery used in your chosen book will act as a guiding compass, because you too have the ability to write wholeheartedly and create an emotive narrative with brilliant, simplistic imagery that hooks your reader in and makes a lasting connection. Use books you love as reference as much as you can. For more on how you can write to connect with your reader, step into the next chapter.

Wholehearted Writing Practice

As a guided practice, I want you to find a book that is closely linked to the book you want to write or are already writing. Read that book from start to finish, or scan if you already know it well. Highlight the moments that make you catch your breath or the imagery that truly resonates. Consider the structure of the book. How many words is it approximately? A good rule of thumb would be to count the words from one full page and times the amount of words on that page, by the number of pages.

If you're looking to write the same sort of thing then it's up to you if you think your story should be shorter or longer. It's up to you how different your story will be.

Once you have a book in mind begin to use it as your guiding compass. Book mark a specific page, if you see fit. And don't feel that you're cheating. Writers have to read. Reading is an essential part of developing your craft. Read and read again, and find that book that will help you to write your story in your way.

Affirmations for Reading with Purpose

The book I need to read is right within my reach.

I find value in reading my favourite books.

Lessons from them come easily and often.

I never have to look far for the right book.

Books are my friend.

I read for joy. I read for purpose.

I am a writer and writers must read.

I read to learn what writing techniques work best for my story.

Chapter 7
Making Wholehearted Connections

"A word after a word after a word is power."
Margaret Atwood

Wholehearted connection is about being authentic in how you present yourself and your story to your reader. It's about choosing the right words, forming the perfect imagery, using a narrative voice that is trustworthy, and that has the ability to speak to readers on a one-to-one level. The way you write and the way it is read could be similar to holding private sessions with each and every reader, if the voice, language and imagery all work together creating that perfect narrative that encapsulates the answers to your audience's needs.

The Right Language

The words you choose to use to convey a problem, or a challenging situation, will make the difference between your readers relating to what you've written and them not connecting. Using words that are familiar to you and your lifestyle/culture and the subject matter is a great place to start. The language you use should come naturally, it shouldn't feel forced or overly-complicated, and as a result, will be easy to understand and resonate with the reader.

A common mistake made by aspiring authors is to use language that isn't familiar to them or their audience. As discussed in the introduction of this book, this results in lost understanding and connection. And I imagine it will make the writing process itself less enjoyable. Put simply, it's a lose-lose scenario.

This may seem obvious, or it may be the first time you're learning that you can write just as you would speak to a friend, and that your book can be made up of familiar language that you and your audience are comfortable with. But I feel it's important to state that the words we use define us. Language is a form of identity. This isn't in the broad sense of say a French speaker speaks French and therefore must either be from France or be connected to the country in a stronger capacity than non-French speakers. Of course, in a broad sense we do identify in just this way, but language gives us other forms of identity. What I'm talking about is the everyday words we use to communicate with our friends, family, children, or work colleagues, or even strangers in the street.

Whether we realise it or not, we identify with others through the language they use. If you think back to having conversations with the people around you or new people you've met – within just a few seconds you made a decision whether you connected to this person, whether you understood them, and if they made sense to you. Some people we just 'get' whilst with others it takes longer to break down who they are and what they're trying to say. This can sometimes be attributed to their vocabulary, whether they like to repeat themselves, or maybe they never get to the point. Perhaps they deliberately keep themselves at a distance by never opening their heart language to anyone. Heart language depicts what is natural and effortless. The language you don't work hard to understand and the language that has the ability to heal, inspire, listen and love. Everyone uses heart language in some way - but some may limit who hears it.

Everyone has a set of vocabulary that they lean

into to express themselves with those closest to them. Pay attention the next time you're having a conversation. Observing this type of exchange will benefit you as a writer. You'll be able to pick up what words are shared without thinking, or those that are pondered on with more consideration to articulate a meaning better. People exchange words without thinking most of the time. Yet, words that are within a heart are sometimes kept locked away thought to be too vulnerable to be allowed to surface.

Try this exercise next time you're with someone close.

This is a word association game. Begin with the word Love. The other person has to say the next word that comes to mind that connects with love. You will then say another word that connects with the last, and the word association game plays out until you feel you've had enough. This should be a fast exercise so that the first thing that comes to mind is said.

The word love will have many related aspects to it. You might find it interesting where the word takes you. You can even begin with the word fear. Fear is another great word to begin this practice. Listen to the words that come out of this play.

You will find with both words, love and fear, that your heart language is ignited. The words that come out are the ones that should be spoken. These will have the ability to reach others with great resonance and connection. If you find your answers to be less reaching, slow the game down and really consider your answer.

This is exactly the same process for writers engaging with readers. Some writers may try to use bigger words than they usually would because that's what they associate with being considered a writer. However, it's important to remember that the key to any writing is keeping the language accessible for your audience. At times, use of larger vocabulary can create a barrier between the story and the storyteller and if there's a disconnect between these two you can guarantee there will be a disconnect between the story and the reader.

I love this next quote because it breathes ease into everything, and yet it's from one of the greatest minds of our time who is renowned for his complexity. Einstein said, 'Make it simple but not simpler.' When telling a story, it's best to keep it in its simplest form. This is not to say that it should be made simpler because others won't understand a more complex version. It means that every element of the story should be considerately unpacked with the attention it deserves. You don't have to group elements of the story together in a complicated fashion. There is no need to rush what you have to say – the beauty of the story is in the detail and you have the right to share everything. It should be presented with language that doesn't have the reader reaching for a dictionary every five minutes. Believe me, this will get old fast as not many readers want to invest that much time and effort, and it will break the flow of the narrative for them. Readers have lots of reasons to pick up a book. Don't let the reason they put yours down be over-complicated language because you were trying to fit an unrealistic and unnecessary idea of how you think you should write into the telling of your story.

Readers want a story in simple language. They don't want to feel that your story and its language is outside of their reach. Easily grasped language means it's easier for the reader to recognise and understand your book's message and learn from it.

Figurative Language and Imagery

One of the great power tools that we writers have locked into our tool belts is imagery through figurative writing. When we want to draw attention to a scene, an object or an emotion we can do this by using the senses through sight, smell, touch, taste and sound which are held together through the imagery a writer creates.

For example, if I wanted to convey an internal feeling of a heart connection between two people it could be articulated in this way:

The touch of his fingertips brushing against my bare skin caught my breath. My heart bungy-jumped from its safe box into the depths of the unknown, where nothing is solid and certain and everything is in motion, moving, falling.

When we use figurative language, we call upon metaphor and simile. These two writing techniques (as mentioned briefly in chapter 6) are power tools that are readily at your disposal. When you want to draw a comparison between two otherwise different objects to give them the same meaning or want to liken one thing to another – these two techniques will help you to successfully make the connection you want to have with the reader. This is the difference between telling the reader and showing your story.

Sometimes it isn't enough to just 'tell' the story especially when we're writing from a place of wholeheartedness. Readers can't see inside your heart unless you show them what it feels like through a visual representation that they can work with.

Whilst both metaphor and simile are of equal measure in their ability to convey meaning, they are different in the way they achieve this:

Simile is a shorter and more direct technique. Here are a few examples so that you know how to recognise them:

His hand was as cold as ice.

The children ran to the chocolate like bees swarm honey.

Simile is when one thing is likened to another. In the examples above we see that the hand is likened to ice, and children have swarmed the chocolate with the precision and focus of bees. The subjects in the beginning, such as the hand and the children, are given an added focus of feeling. The hand is frozen. The children's excitement.

Metaphor or extended metaphor can create a longer version that allows the writer to say one thing IS another. Emotion or state of being can be conveyed in this way. Take T.S. Eliot's *The Waste Land*. This is a true depiction of how extended metaphor is successfully used. Eliot conveys the sadness of the lives lost to war and the confusion of new life that spring offers.

> *"April is the cruellest month breeding*
>
> *Lilacs out of the dead land,*
>
> *mixing Memory and desire,*
>
> *stirring dull roots with spring rain."*

Metaphor is used in this instance to invoke thought from its reader. Each line builds from the last creating a greater picture. The language creates power over the reader as it invites them to consider the death that lies beneath the soil and how difficult it is to celebrate new beginnings of spring and new life amongst what has been lost. The unforgiving nature of a new spring comes regardless.

The imagery you choose should always be relatable to the context of the story and to your audience's ability to relate. When you want to describe a moment through imagery, consider what is happening at the time and the way you want the reader to feel when they picture your words.

Your Writing Voice

Voice is 'the' most important element of your storytelling strategy for your book. Your writing voice is the one aspect that will draw a reader in from the very first sentence.

Are you wondering how you know which is the best writing voice for you? Every writer goes through the same thought process and it's fair to say, that in every book you write, you'll be asking the same question of yourself in the beginning. If you know your book's purpose and you know your reader well, the tone of your voice and the way you address the subject with the reader will come naturally. Every story is different and therefore it's always good to check in and experiment with the voice that best represents the story. Just like heart language, there's also heart voice.

After all, what is a voice without heart? Where is the passion? Where is the fear? Where does the desire sit? It's always good to realign. Whether this is your first book or your seventh. You should still ask this question to make sure that your story is being told in the best wholehearted way, in that it is told right from the heart, in a way perfect for your audience.

I find that the voice that I'm most comfortable with is the one that comes most naturally. The one that you don't have to work hard to maintain. The one that flows with ease. The one that sometimes you don't want anyone to hear. In the same way that you breathe in air and exhale without much thought – this is how your natural writing voice will feel to you.

A good way of finding your voice is to just write and see how that translates on paper, as well as, how easy it feels to release what's in your heart.

For some, this voice will be conversational, colloquial, or both. It will be like talking to your reader as if you're chatting to a friend. Perhaps the closest of friends with a language that only you two share.

You can either choose to use the I voice (first-person), or the he/she (third-person) approach.

First person is known as the 'I' voice. You will refer to self as I, me, we, mine, my.

For example:

'There's so much I want to tell you.' (first-person)

For other writers, a third person voice will feel more comfortable. This might read like: 'There are three things that she will learn from this book.' (third- person)

A third person voice uses pronouns such as 'he, she, we, them, they, their'. It will be telling the story from an observed point of view, and will also create an element of detachment that feels different in the narrative to when the I voice is used. But if third-person is done well, and depending on subject matter, it doesn't have to detract from the wholehearted writing method. You can still write from the heart in third-person. Though if you're writing a self-improvement book or memoir, I would suggest using first-person as the 'I voice' has greater personality and connection for this style of book. You are telling your story, after all.

Whilst there are choices in selecting the right writing voice, it should always be authentic to you as the writer and be chosen only because it's the best voice that will achieve maximum connection with your reader. Don't be afraid to write in the most familiar way that comes to you. This voice might be the perfect voice that creates the strongest wholehearted connections, and you won't find that out until you experiment with both. So, get writing and play around with what comes naturally to you.

Wholehearted Writing Practice

Consider the language you use when speaking to people on a daily basis. Start paying attention to the language other people use and how you relate and connect to that language. Make notes on your findings. What common words do you find your friends using?

Have a go at developing imagery using simile or metaphor or both. Take a look at the examples given in the chapter and use these as guide to steer you in the right direction.

Starting now, begin to write. Play around with a pencil and a piece of paper or grab a laptop or even a smart phone and start identifying with your writing voice. If one voice doesn't feel comfortable, try another. Switch between a first person (I voice) and a third person (he, she, they voice) to see which better connects with you.

Affirmations for Connection

I connect with my reader through my heart voice.

I connect with my reader through my heart language.

My heart language is the same as my reader's heart language.

I am safe to share my heart language with my readers.

I connect with my reader through my story.

I am connected to my heart voice.

I am connected to my heart language.

I am connected to my reader.

The imagery I use to show my reader is relatable to them.

Chapter 8
Expand the Flow of Creativity

"The more of me I be, The clearer I can see."
Rachel Andrews

Firstly, setting the intention to write your book will lead to a path of commitment. Did you know that 80% of the world's population say they're going to write a book? And can you guess how many of that 80% actually do? Just 1%.

Surprised? I was. But then, when I set the intention to do something, I do it. It's easy for me to think that everyone is the same. And, honestly, I think a lot of people are the same. There's a host of reasons why those 79% of people who want to write a book, never do: time, courage, knowing how, confidence. A few of those reasons will have hopefully been addressed in the earlier chapters of this book.

Mindset is likely to be the number one set-back

that stops aspiring writers from achieving author status. Mindset that is underpinned by self-doubt, lack of worth, and underestimated value will prevent even the most talented writers from writing. But all this really is, is negative self-talk and old thoughts which can be replaced with new ones that support the dream of writing your book.

The next reason on this list is intention. Setting the intention of "I'll write a book one day" is not setting an intention at all. It's establishing a dream with no clear path to follow, and so it remains a dream, somewhere painted in the distant future; a day that will never quite materialise – unless you commit.

Setting clear steps for you to move forward with the determination to write that book is how the 1% actually find the purpose, time, drive, and motivation to get that book written, to get the dream ticked off, and to get that goal accomplished. Every step of this journey is you becoming a better writer and owning your craft.

In order to match that intention with actual action, you need to establish a writing routine and carve out time in your day, every day. But remember, as with all goals, they need to be broken down into small, manageable and maintainable steps.

Outlining the content for your book in detail will help you to plan your book from beginning to end. You can apply a timeline to writing each section which will give you a schedule of how long it will take to write your book. This means that you always have the end in sight. You have the vision of your completed manuscript in your fingertips. It will not be a pipedream that is a never-ending cycle of effort and no reward. Intention, planning and action will make sure you achieve what you set out to do. Without fail.

This will not only help you keep the goal in sight, it will also help you prioritise when other commitments pop up and pull you away. And when this does happen, which invariably it will, don't panic, you've got this. With planning and scheduling – time is your friend. With this knowledge, it's easy to move things along with a clear plan of what needs to happen, allowing you to adjust and move forward.

The bugbear that I hear a lot is that new writers don't want to share their dream of writing a book with friends and family. Probably because they don't want to become a part of that statistic that resolves so many into letting go of that dream and never acting on it. That 79% statistic has a lot to answer for. Yet, believe it or not, there is power in sharing your intention. Making it known to family and friends and the people in your life can actually be helpful.

Once you have a vision for your book, and your holding its purpose firm in your grasp, you can share that vision and your plan of how you're going to make it happen with your friends, family and the people you count on, and who count on you. It's also interesting that from the people we expect to receive most judgement from, they usually surprise us, by sharing a great enthusiasm that helps to realise your dream. By sharing your dream you're opening up the channel of creative flow. That could be creating more time, patience, support, and of course the creativity involved in the process of writing your book.

This too comes from wholehearted sharing – sharing from the heart. Don't forget that 80% of the entire population of the world say they want to write a book, and this statistic could well include several of the people closest to you. Without you even realising, you could be sharing your dream with a loved one who had the same goal. You sharing your intention, could ignite their own dream once again. They'll either be happy to help you make yours come true, or use your commitment and dedication as inspiration to pick their dream up from where they left it. If this happens, you have a sense of community spirit to work with.

Give those close to you a vision of the steps you have planned. The planning of the book. The outlining of the plot. The conflict and resolution. The problem your book is addressing and the purpose of your story. Let them know about the best how-to-guide or memoir or work of fiction that's going to be written this year. By you! Confidence is key. Believe in yourself and others with follow. Your excitement and determination will be infectious.

Share with them the reason you're writing this book. Explain how your audience needs this. Sell the book's purpose to them and educate them on the market for such a book. And remember, ideas lead to more ideas. One creative mind communicating with another may open a channel of creativity that you never thought possible. The more you share with other people, the more you might get in return.

Visualising all this means that not only will you

be demonstrating your strategy to achieve your goal, you'll be establishing the steps and the processes that need to take place to actualise it and make it happen every step of the way. From preparation to planning, from plotting to character building, from writing chapter to chapter, from meeting audience demands to knowing where your audience hangs out are all crucial elements of the process. All these elements will demonstrate that this is more than just a pipe dream. This is a strategy with clear defined steps that will lead you to your goal. And if you share your plan to write this book with your people, you may even have a cheerleading squad showing up at moments when you really need the motivation and belief.

Having a vision of getting to the end of your book, and how your readers will engage with it, is the encouragement every writer needs. Visualisation will help with self-doubt and negative self-talk. Be mindful and keep focused on the WHY and getting to the end – and trust me - you will get there.

Having set the intention and created a space to write, it's worth recognising that there may be moments when you need to switch off and relax in order for your creativity to flow abundantly.

Whether it's the creativity of language, imagery, plot twists, conveying a concept, or articulating a moment, you have to learn to be kind to yourself and the creative process that comes with it, so that you are within a writing practice that works for you. Ideas and new ways of describing things can take time to be born from your heart voice and your heart language. Channelling the right words is achieved through a place of mental calmness and relaxation. To achieve this state of mind and to give the very best of you to your writing practice, don't be afraid to take a break and do something fun.

You could go to the movies and get lost in someone else's story. I personally love this one. I have had many an "AHA" moment whilst relaxing at the cinema. I often find going to the movies a great source of inspiration because my mind is totally free from my story, relaxed and in a place of rest. I'm having fun. I'm entertained and I'm open to anything.

You could walk to your favourite place in a local forest. There's a woodland close to where I live that I've visited since I was a child. For me, there is nothing like being immersed in the sound of nature: the energetic flow of a waterfall crashing into a rock pool, birdsong, the scent of fresh pine. These are all the things that bring me peace and allow me to escape from the hustle of my mind and everyday commitments that can sometimes limit my creative flow. Another thing that brings me great peace is a clear star-filled night sky. This relaxes me so much all my fears just fall away.

I never allow myself to be blocked. I recognise that I'm stalling way before a block happens. I recognise I need a break and need to re-connect with myself and my heart. Once I do this, I create a space for a free-flowing expansion of creativity. For me, I already know that all the answers I will ever need are already within me. I know that all I need to do is quiet my mind and connect with other people or other things for the answer to be triggered. This has happened so often that I no longer fear not knowing because I know the answer will come to me at the right time. It will always come in one way or another. Always.

Have this faith too and your flow of creativity will never falter, which means you will never fall away from the heart of writing your book, and you will always reach your goal of writing those final words of your story.

Wholehearted Writing Practice

Today is about setting your intention. You need to establish who your reader is and where you will find them. Your intention should meet their need. Do some research. Your book is not just for you – it is for them. Your audience. Seek them out. Hold them tight. Learn everything you can about them and combine this understanding within your story.

Establish a writing practice that will work for you. You could set up an hour a day for planning, writing, researching, or you could set up 3 hours a day depending on your other work/life commitments. Once you commit and set the intention, your determination will be proven in the actions you take. Have all this in place and the book will take care of itself.

Finally, let it be known. Don't be afraid to tell those close to you what your intention is. Open a channel of creativity between you and your supporters.

Step out into a place that makes you happy. Let your mind be clear. Let your breath soften and your shoulders relax. You are opening the creative channel between your heart and soul.

This is your chance to just be. Let creativity flow through you. When you're ready, find somewhere to write and download all the thoughts and ideas that come freely.

Once you share your intention, dedication, plans, and audience, it will not only invite others to share it, it makes the process real. Creating reality for you as a writer is so important. You are a writer. It's more than OKAY to call yourself a writer. You have permission to become an author An author who relates, inspires and leads.

With these intentions, little by little, you will move toward something great, until one day, you're looking back with pride thinking "I did that".

Affirmations for Creative Flow

I am one with my creative flow.

Creativity flows through me abundantly.

I am creativity.

I am in the perfect space to clear my mind for creative abundance to flow.

My heart language and heart voice are filled with creative flow.

I open creative channels with people close to me, and new channels of creativity open to support me.

People surprise me every day in their willingness to support me and connect their creative flow to mine.

Cheryl Hart

Chapter 9
Cultivating a Leader Spirit

"Do not judge me by my successes, judge me by how many times I fell down and got back up again."

Nelson Mandela

Stand guarded and you'll be unreachable. Stand with your arms open wide and you'll create an open space to embrace those reading your story. You will become a trusted leader through the honesty you share and your commitment to telling your story through vulnerability, courage and authenticity.

Sometimes, when we've been through a challenging experience, we forget that we may still be wearing the armour that we put on to protect us from harm during that moment in our lives. If you recognise this could be you or has been you, don't worry as the armour we equip ourselves with is a perfectly natural instinctual form of defence. But a leader is not respected alone through their strength and knowledge – a leader must show how they came to be in their position and share what they have learnt.

After a challenging life event or situation, it goes against our survival instincts to drop this armour and let our barriers down all at once. Our survival instincts are what have protected us, and those same survival instincts will need reassurance that it's a safe environment to be free within and be true to who we are once more. It's also natural that we will have changed during the process of our experiences. Often, we grow more resilient, wiser, stronger, smarter, and perhaps more cautious and controlled in certain ways.

We may even be perceived as distant, until we have assessed a new environment, and evaluated all corners of this new territory safe. We may have learned that to be cautious pays off. We may have adopted new behaviours that keep us safe, healthy or positive. We will, beyond doubt, have changed in some way, and this is okay, in fact, it's a natural process in the evolution of humanology. We experience, we adapt, we change, and the cycle continues to repeat.

Yet, what we must not do is keep people at arm's length. We must re-connect to our core spirit of what makes us who we are, because regardless of what we have experienced, the person we started out as is as deserving of love and acceptance as the person that stands before you in the mirror today. Being a butterfly writer is about acknowledging lessons, vulnerability and strengths and imparting this wisdom.

It's worth taking a moment to recognise, that the many selves you have been in your life, all make up the whole person you are today. The writer spirit within you will need to connect with all of these past selves so that you can share your heart through empathy, compassion and understanding for the many readers that may be walking in your old shoes, and to do this, you must first do a mental check to see if you are wearing any emotional armour that will restrict the way you connect with your reader.

Okay, so how do you check if your barriers are still up before you get down to writing a book? To share what you've learnt so that your story helps, heals, inspires or entertains, you need to be open with them. How do you really know if you're guarding part of yourself from unseen threats and keeping your heart protected. How do you really know that your audience will welcome you warmly?

Answer the following questions as honestly as you can from the multiple choice answers given below:

1. How do you own your story?

- I share it with grace and gratitude. I understand what that moment taught me and what place it played in my life. I respect the value.
- I like talking about it.
- I avoid talking about it.
- I share some points with others and hold some back.
- I'm particular with who I share my story with.

2. How do you feel when you think of the challenges you have faced?

- Resentment
- Remorse
- Courage
- Pride
- Vulnerability

- Sadness
- Neglect
- Horror
- Torment
- Fear
- Gratitude
- Peace

3. How have the challenges/experiences impacted your life?

- I'm in a healthier place because of them.
- They held me back from becoming something more.
- I feel awakened.
- I am blocked, stuck and limited because of them; unable to move forward.
- I am reaching my full potential.

4. Do you consider your challenges moments of growth that allow you to explore your strength and purpose in life?

- Yes
- No

Recognising the way you feel about your story can be an excellent guidepost in making you aware of any resentment, fear and loss that may still be lurking beneath the surface. Not dealing with these emotions can result in you telling your story in the wrong way. Delivering the right message, with the right words, in the right tone is the difference between embracing your reader with love and hope, and keeping your reader at a distance. Never penetrating their heart with your story is the result in keeping your heart under lock and key.

Since you've come this far through the narrative of this book, learning how to connect with your story, your reader, your heart language and your heart voice, it would be an oversight not to check in with yourself, after doing all this work, and release any blocks that may still be there that will prevent you from writing from the heart.

Let's take a look at your answers from the questions above.

If you answered b, c, or d in question 1 then

you may be carrying feelings of shame about an experience; fear that has not been eliminated, regret that you could have done something differently, or worry that it's all going to happen again. You may even be concerned that in some way your readers will not understand your heart, your actions, your responses and who you are today. Let me tell you right now, if this is you in any way, you firstly have the right to feel all the things you feel. Secondly, you have the right to use any or all of these emotions to connect with your reader. If done in the right way – these are wonderful elements to present to your reader as these represent you and your story as honest and relatable.

It might be worthwhile addressing any of these emotions before you begin to write the story, so that you turn these emotions from blocks disconnecting you from telling your story with heart, into the fuel that fuses connection. This is turning your vulnerability into courage, that courage into confidence, and all of these elements into deep connections with your reader.

This feels like the perfect time to remind yourself that everything that happens has a consequence. Just like the law of cause and effect. We take on challenges and experiences, and are thrust into situations that trigger a reaction in our external world, which then triggers a reaction within our internal one, the heart.

It can be a helpful exercise when becoming aware of emotions within the body to write them down. For example: when thinking of moments from your past; a tight chest can signal anxiety or a rapid heartbeat can point to fear induced by the adrenaline from that thought. The emotions may not always be so obvious at first but as you become aware of the body's behaviour and how it's reacting to a thought, you can begin to understand the emotion behind it. Just one thought can cause a physical reaction. It's worthwhile to become aware of how powerful this can be.

The information you're looking for may not come all at once, so if you've picked up a pen to begin to write and nothing is coming up for you, that's okay. Just be mindful that something may be lurking beneath the surface, and leave the gate open. Become more alert and enable yourself to sit with emotions, and reflect. To question where that feeling is coming from is the first step in understanding your heart. When you understand your heart, you can teach it to others, and when others can learn from you, you have cultivated a leader spirit.

Getting to know your heart can be learning to have a dialogue with it. This doesn't need to be something you write in twenty minutes. It could take you a lot longer to learn how to do this. You could keep adding to what you learn as and when you become aware of something.

Stay with it so that you are learning what that emotion has to offer you, and whether this emotion is holding you back.

Before we continue, I want you to be mindful of the purpose of this exercise, because when you're aware of all the emotions that reside within you, you also become aware of any armour or barriers you have put up when you feel yourself resisting things. Then you are able to identify the possible reasons behind this resistance. This self-analysis puts you in a strong position when writing for your reader, as you're able to tell your story through the heart of someone who feels their way through life and learns every step of the way.

I want you to consider the journey or story that

you wish to share with your reader and recount the sequence of events from where you are now, to where it all began; carefully moving back in time, noting all the shifts in action and how you felt during those times, and comment on the triggers that moved you from one stage of the journey to the next.

We often say that hindsight is a beautiful thing, well this exercise will allow you to walk through your journey collecting the elements of hindsight that will give you a deeper understanding of how you got from the beginning to the now, and how you evolved as a person and have come to the position of sharing your story.

Before you begin, I want to assure you that this doesn't have to be a complicated exercise. There may seem like many moments that contributed to this experience, maybe too many to list, but once you begin to see the points in front of you, you may start to see that some of these points can be grouped together as episodes within your story.

After all, things don't typically just happen 'out of the blue' - there is usually a myriad of moments that build up to the experience.

Being rooted in the present will make it emotionally healthier for you to reach back into the experience to get what you need to tell your story with all your heart, without getting stuck in the past, which can be psychologically challenging and delay your progress. Keeping an anchor in the present whilst creating a timeline of events will also help you to appreciate how much you have evolved and the strength of your person. The timeline will also serve you well when it comes to choosing the right structure for your book and deciding upon the best way to tell your story, so that it has the most positive effect on the reader's journey.

When you can see how these events triggered moments of action or shifts of perspective for you, you may also become aware of your personal growth, and how these events triggered a stronger sense of self and self-worth and self-value. And when you realise these aspects of yourself (regardless of the difficulties and challenges that you have faced) you may also be able to see how the shame, vulnerability and fear, lose their power over you. In fact, you then have the power to turn them from negatives into positives. From vulnerability to courage. You can then begin to feel empowered by your story and all that it involves; the good, the bad, the ugly, the beautiful, the vulnerability and the courage. Everything within you is what makes you who you are. So what if you felt fearful in the past (and might still sometimes), we all feel fear. So what if you lost your courage along the way (we all do). It's this rawness that makes you real, relatable and altogether human.

For each of you that answered A to question one, I would suggest still doing the timeline trigger in recounting events and documenting the feelings associated with them as directed earlier in this chapter. Doing these exercises are never a waste of time, even if you think you have everything you need, an exercise like this might uncover just one more thing that will make your story more wholehearted, and with that, you can guarantee more wholehearted connections with your readers, and with that, you can guarantee a lifelong community of like-for-like hearts.

If you answered feelings such as fear, resentment, or anger in question 2 – these leak negativity into your thought patterns which will incite negative emotion. Negative emotion should not power your heart voice when writing to your reader. Yes, by all means talk about how these feelings came up for you at some point, but feelings of hostility should be worked through before directing your story at your reader. A leader has already dealt with the hard stuff. A leader leads through compassion and the knowledge of the strength of all they've learned, and how they will lead through such wisdom.

Question two is all about honesty and finding out which emotions are still triggered by your experience. You can still be working on them, that's absolutely fine. But be sure to be aware of them if you are. Awareness and acknowledging emotions that still trigger you allow you to make the room to accept the situation and grow from it. If you're still feeling pain, acknowledge it. It might be that you've made peace with much of your past and that you're still working on one or two aspects. If you acknowledge it, the negativity won't bleed into your heart voice. Instead, your heart voice will be filled with compassion and patience for yourself, and your reader will feel this.

Question three. If you're writing a story about an event in your life – whether this be dressed up as fiction or laid bare in non-fiction – you will need to have recognised the power of that event. How have you grown? How have you developed? Or how is your character going to develop through this experience as you put them through each event. With each experience there is an element of growth, be it fiction or non-fiction, the result is the same. Growth happens in both worlds. You need to be aware of how you've grown, so that you can show the reader a natural progression of awareness and acceptance. Using events as fuel to develop the person or character you're writing about is exactly how you should be looking at events. Ask yourself: How did I grow from this? Or, how does my character grow from this?

If you consider your experience as lessons for you to grow and lead, the question to answer 4 will be 'Yes'. You will easily find your purpose and that purpose will channel your heart into a book. If you have answered 'No' to this question, you'll need to focus your energy on learning what your experiences have to offer you and your reader before beginning to write your story.

Conflict and Resolution

Timeline triggers are a wonderful way of assigning feelings to events so that you can draw from them at later stages in your book. Note, that when you assign a negative emotion such as sadness, fear or loss, that this in literary terms is 'conflict'.

Conflict often occurs when some other party wants something from you that you're not prepared to give or that you feel jeopardised in giving. Conflict can spread over long periods of time or shorter moments. Regardless of the conflict, there will always be resolution that follows. At first, the resolution might be an action that keeps the peace, returning a situation to a calmer, bearable environment. However, at some point that same conflict may rise again, and again, and again, each time it being resolved to a satisfactory level but never being fully resolved, so that it builds with ebb and flow, until reaching its final point in conflict where the climactic resolution is found. Take a look at the diagram below for an idea of how conflict and resolution might look. The high points reflect the drama and conflict, the low points reflect moments of calm and resolution. There are times when the points of conflict might rise higher than others, and moments where the peace and resolution may occur for longer.

Conflict

Resolution

When you assign a positive feeling to an event such as peace, joy, achievement, this is what is termed 'resolution'. As mentioned above resolution follows conflict. This could be a family argument that occurs at every family reunion, or a boss that is relentless on making your life hell. Whilst the drama will be swept up in the conflict, it's important to note that

drama is woven into resolution. For example: The largely 'put-on' designated family cook has the last laugh by adding dog food to the beef stew; or the boss from hell is found in a compromising position with an intern introducing vulnerability and a motive to let-up on who they've been victimising. Each of these scenarios produce a moment of reprieve and even joy for a character. Conflict and resolution can go on and on and on.

The trick is that each time conflict is raised something happens that shifts the story forward increasing the impact of conflict, the need for peace, and the call for a more permanent resolve.

Understanding the push and pull effect of cause and effect, and bad vs good, will give you a clearer understanding of your journey and how you should lead your story as well as realising all the wins you had along the way, no matter how small or how insignificant they may have seemed at the time. They were all connecting to the big win, the game changer, and therefore, they all count.

Think Things Through

For those of you who consider your life being worse because of the events you've experienced, then maybe you're not yet ready to tell your story

because you're not completely out the other side. Maybe you're still living it in some small way. Maybe you're still feeling the vibrations of the impact. This too is perfectly fine as the right time and place to tell your story will present itself.

You may still be processing and allowing all the resolution to fall into place. Just when you think that a moment of conflict is over, BAM! It starts up again, right? It happens. So don't worry, simply observe. Do the exercises laid out in this book and work through your journey and all that's involved.

Make notes in a journal and have faith that good things will happen. Set the intention to write your story but perhaps write it for you to begin with so that you learn, discover, and evolve through the writing process. There may be much you need to learn about how you've grown, what you can share to lead others, and how your heart has the power to connect with vulnerability to create courage.

I promise you, if you do this, you will emerge an author empowered by your journey, and then you'll want to write it for others to read and learn from, or entertain or inspire. Be ready to see the good in everything. Be ready to feel transformation take place.

If you consider yourself ready now to write your story, to tackle everything and get it all out, then this next practice is really going to get you off to a flying start.

Being a Butterfly Writer is about aligning yourself with what you know, discovering the strength in that knowledge, and sharing it with your readers.

Once you have this firm in your grasp, take flight with it and make sure your wisdom reaches those who need it.

Wholehearted Guided Practice

Get comfortable, grab a pencil and paper and write down all the aspects of your journey that have taught you something. If you can, make a note of the moments when you decided you wanted change, then write down what inspired you to connect to this change. Knowing this may help you know what to write to encourage others to do the same, or you might discover points in which your reader can relate to your story. It's these events that create moments of epiphany for your readers. Remember to take it easy, don't force it, allow your heart to guide you. It will give you the information with ease, if you take your time and let it flow naturally.

Recognising the power in these moments and the process of understanding is what makes you a leader.

Affirmations for Leadership

I am a leader.

I lead others to understand how they can activate change for themselves.

I am at peace with all my history. What is not yet resolved within, I am aware of and working to accept.

My leadership skills grow day by day. When I realise another goal I have achieved, I grow stronger to lead with certainty.

My heart voice is compassionate and strong.

My heart language is encouraging and warm.

I am honest and authentic. I am everything a leader should be.

I am a butterfly writer ready to impart wisdom, connection and relatability into the hearts of my readers.

Next Steps for Wholehearted Writing

1. Get comfortable with being vulnerable.

2. Get confident and invoke courage.

3. Turn negative, limiting thoughts into positive, nourishing ones.

4. Know your audience and establish their needs.

5. Make the wholehearted connection through reading, your audience and within your heart.

6. Let your readers see your vulnerabilities and your courage.

7. Write from the heart knowing that like-minded hearts will read your work with relief and joy.

8. Write simply and clearly.

9. Set the intention to finish your book. Visualise the outcome, the end, and the publication date.

10. Let your intention be known.

Writing a book could be the most rewarding action you take. Write wholeheartedly and you will guarantee that your effort will be read in a wholehearted way establishing a connection with your reader that goes beyond just words on a page.

THE AUTHOR Programme

Transform Yourself into an Author with Purpose, Connection and Wisdom

If you're ready to recognise your worth and the value of your story, and want to develop it into a book (whether for the open market or just for you) The Author Programme is the perfect partner to make your vision a reality.

Like others before you, you can turn your experience into a book with the proven methodology and unwavering support of The Author Programme. The programme, brought to you by The Academy of Writers, will guide you step-by-step through it's easy to read guidance and writing practices, printed and bound in a lever file for tangible, easy use.

The result of completing this programme depends entirely on you. You may find you've written your first draft before you finish the course, or you may choose to take it slower. You will be in complete control of what you write, when you write and how you write it. You will be in the company of those who have walked in your shoes and believe in your ability to achieve your goal. Support is given to understand the value in your story, as and when you need it.

Visit **www.theauthorprogramme.com** to find out how you can become the next debut author. I promise, you'll be in safe hands.

You are worthy. You can do this. Your time is now.

www.theauthorprogramme.com

If you've enjoyed reading this book then please leave a review. This book was written to help aspiring authors believe they can write a book and become an author.

If this book has given you even the smallest inspiration that you have the value necessary to become an author with purpose, connection and wisdom then spread the word by leaving a review, tell your friends and anyone you encounter that feels the desire to write.

The more writers that discover their worth, value and wisdom, the better connected we'll all be.

With love,

Cheryl

Cheryl Hart
Founder of The Academy of Writers
and The Author Programme.

Printed in Great Britain
by Amazon